Photo by Leonel Carlos Valle

A scene from the HERE production of "Moose Mating." Set design by Leonel Carlos Valle.

MOOSE
MATING

BY DAVID GRAE

★

★

DRAMATISTS
PLAY SERVICE
INC.

MOOSE MATING
Copyright © 1996, David Grae

All Rights Reserved

SPECIAL NOTE

SPECIAL NOTE ON SONGS AND RECORDINGS

Thanks Mom

MOOSE MATING was produced by David Grae and premiered at the Club Space at HERE in New York City on July 20, 1995. It was directed and choreographed by Annie Loui; the set and lighting designs were by Leonel C. Valle; the costume design was by Melissa Toth; the original music was composed and performed by Andy Boehmke; the percussionist was Matthew Jorgensen and the stage manager was Emily Orr. The cast was as follows:

NARRATOR .... David Greenspan
BETSY .... Johnna Schmidt
LONNIE/CABBY .... Ben Shenkman
MICHAEL .... Ron Bagden
JOSIE .... Lydia Radziul

CHARACTERS

Betsy — twenties/early thirties
Michael — twenties/early thirties
Lonnie — twenties/early thirties
Josie — twenties/early thirties
Narrator — ageless

Only five actors needed, or four if the Narrator is recorded.

Smaller parts to be doubled into main players:

Cabby — a foreigner, can be played by actor playing Lonnie,
    Narrator or Josie
Offstage Voices — can be played by any actor or stagehand
    who happens to be offstage at the time
Baseball Announcer — can be played by actor playing Narra-
    tor, Lonnie or Josie, or a recorded voice

SETTING

New York City. Present.

AUTHOR'S NOTE

I offer these thoughts to help you prepare a production of the play. They are meant to relay my intentions while writing the play and what I thought worked in its first production in New York City at the HERE theater. However, you may have far greater insights than I into what makes the play work on stage. Take away what you like and scrap the rest....

I wrote the play to be performed with music and choreographed movement. The Asides and the Narrator's passages are the most logical sections to be stylized with music and movement. I see the longer Asides and Narrator speeches working much as songs work in a musical — they take a step out of reality, into thoughts and sub-textual feelings. I intended a stark difference between the naturalistic scenes and the Asides and Narrator monologues.

In the HERE theater production, this division of realities, which was augmented by lighting shifts and amplifying the Narrator's voice, helped to create a wonderful sense of playfulness and theatricality. The director was also a professional choreographer and the composer not only created the music but performed it live on piano along with a percussionist. I can imagine recorded music working as well, but there is something nice about live music in the live theater. It's organic. And because we had a live musician, he also provided live sound effects, including ringing phones, call waiting tones and doorbells. The only recording was the background sound of the baseball game.

There are also sections without text that require movement and music, such as the scene where Michael and Betsy read together then make love. Simple choreography accompanied by romantic music made for a lovely sequence in the HERE theater production. Later in the play, after Michael and Betsy have an argument, heavy electric guitar and a driving rock beat created the jagged atmosphere for a choreographed dance-fight between the two lovers.

Although a prop plot is provided, you can easily perform the show without props and have the actors mime them. In the HERE theater production, we used several choice props — Betsy's duffel bag, scrap of paper, pen, football, books, TV remote control and phones — and mimed the others. For instance, the bong, which could have potentially become problematic, was simply mimed. Same with the video game joystick. The audience didn't seem to mind at all.

As for the set, a bare stage with a scrim was quite effective. Three colorful, sturdy chairs carried on and off by the actors throughout the performance were the only real set pieces. In the first restaurant scene, two chairs were enough to suggest the atmosphere. There was no need to haul out a table. Michael and Betsy's thoughts were projected above their heads onto the scrim. The taxi cab was created with three chairs placed in a column. When Betsy called for a cab, the actor playing the Cabby dashed out and set the chairs. The chairs didn't move once set; the actors did, suggesting the movement of the cab. For example, when the cab hit a bump, the three actors popped up and down in their chairs. Turns were created by the actors leaning to one side. This simplicity went a long way in keeping the performance moving with no pauses for set changes.

The scrim provided more than just a screen for the text of Michael and Betsy's thoughts. The scrim was backlit during the Narrator's long speech about Michael's dream; the actors playing Lonnie and Josie performed a shadow dance as Michael and Betsy slept in one another's arms on stage. Another effective use of the scrim was during Betsy's monologue near the end of the play when Michael and Lonnie are skydiving. Again, a backlit scrim provided just the right touch to see Michael and Lonnie shadow-skydive; music imitating the furious roar of a single-engine plane completed the atmosphere.

The entire play should be performed as one continuous action with no act break. However, if your theater requires an act break, then Act One should end with: "JOSIE and LONNIE ... PLAY THE GAME!" (page 34 of this edition). Scenes should flow seamlessly into one another without interruption. Dialogue cues from one scene to the next should, in most cases, be picked up immediately, even when actors from the previous scene are still on stage. Musical riffs and crossfading lights can instantly indicate passage of time and change of locale.

I owe thanks to several wonderful friends and family members who helped make MOOSE MATING a reality. Barry Kenyon, my screenwriting partner, helped edit the first fifteen or so pages of the script. Jamie Heller lent great insight into relationships through her own scholarship on the subject and countless hours of discourse. Steve Killebrew was the first to sit me down for a serious discussion about animal mating habits. My grandmother Eve and my grandfather Hy, still in love after more than sixty years of marriage, taught me about compassion. Peter Rini introduced me to two fifths of the original cast. Jeff Fligelman, my business partner at Gotham Writers' Workshop, provided unfailing support, especially when my head was immersed in the play and not our business. Jed "Mr. Reliable" Weissberg took time out to snap publicity shots. Johnna Schmidt and Annie Loui, from first to final draft, offered invaluable script notes. Annie directed and choreographed the original production with brilliance beyond my own vision. Of course, she couldn't have done it without the incredibly talented cast, designers, stage manager and musicians to whom I am indebted for their hard work and dedication. And, hey, while I'm at it, thanks Mom, Dad, Seth and Marlena.

N.Y.C.
May, 1996

David Grae

MOOSE MATING

At rise: Stage in darkness. Main musical theme plays for a few bars. Then we see the Narrator.

NARRATOR.   The story of Betsy and Michael begins at a play downtown in Manhattan. A monologue by Lonnie Goldman. Betsy is in the midst of her performance ... *(Sudden flash of light reveals Betsy on a bare stage.)*
BETSY.   ... and I'm in a sea, a fog, a miasma of rugs and tables and authors and Chaucer and cranberries and fruits and gays and Fred Astaire and movies and Reagan and Bush and pussy and dogs and blindness and Oedipus and Rex Harrison and Dolly and pulleys and paisleys and buildings and Ring-Dings and dicks and pricks and Daryl and robes and Daryl and dangling and dicks and pricks and lips and all I want to do is ejaculate but I can't because I'm a woman! *(Different music fades up as lights fade to black on Betsy. Beat. The sound of applause. Lights flash up again. Exhausted, Betsy bows several times mouthing, "Thank you. Thank you very much." Michael, who has been in the audience, stands and applauds.)*
MICHAEL.   Author! Author! *(Betsy gestures toward the wings.)*
BETSY.   Lonnie! C'mon Lonnie! C'mon. *(Lonnie Goldman bashfully walks out and bows to a swell of applause and screaming fans. Betsy claps. To audience.)* Lonnie Goldman! *(Betsy hugs him. They bow together then leave the stage. Some indication of time passing with music and a light shift. Betsy returns with a large duffel bag slung over her shoulder.)*
OFFSTAGE VOICE.   Great show, Betsy.
BETSY.   Thanks, Hank. See you tomorrow. *(Betsy bumps into Michael. Big movement here, not naturalism. Aside.)* Shit, he's cute.
MICHAEL.   *(Aside.)* Wow. I feel chemistry here. I mean I feel the possibility of an absence. Like cold is the absence of heat? Or is it absinthe? No. Absence. The absence of misery, loneliness, suffering. The chance to *not* wake up hugging dreams

of my sweet ex Lisa. Seven fucking years ago, destroyed me and left me shopping for fruit alone at four in the morning and going to these fucking plays at all hours. I hate plays that I don't star in. It's just the hope of maybe bumping into a beautiful woman that keeps me coming back and back for months, years already and now, right now, she is next to me. I've actually achieved the unachievable: I HAVE MET A WOMAN AT A PLAY. Or at least I've had physical contact even if it's only inadvertent, which is *something* anyway, better than staring blankly across a room desperately trying to think of what to say, anything, "Hi," "Hello," "Hey," "Hi, I'm Michael," "Hey, how ya doin'?" "Hello, I'm Michael, pretty cool place, huh?" "What are you drinking?" "I just wanted to tell you that you have beautiful hair," "You know where the bathroom is?" And then working up the guts till my throat hurts to actually approach a woman, only to find I don't have the guts to approach her, and then watching her walk away without any indication that she saw me, heard me, smelled me, or felt my presence in any way — hundreds, thousands of women, maybe millions who stirred my libido, tickled my loins, pricked my prick at parties, bars, in the park, on the street, subways, buses, boats, airplanes, movies, restaurants, elevators, miniature golf courses, parks, sports arenas, stores, malls, gymnasiums, concerts, everywhere, all around the world, my imaginary romances with them all, making sweet tender love, my blissful moments of fantasy, my enduring hope and everlasting passion. But now, THIS, ACTUAL CONTACT, A BUMP, A LOVELY BUMP, *this* must be fate or some unearthly cosmic force and I'm petrified, terrified, wondrafied, and I'm floating, dazed, drunk, I think I'm hyperventilating, suddenly I love my miserable lonely life, I'm inspired, I love humanity and trees and architecture, I want to donate blood, I want to fight for the environment ... and the universe, the sadness and all the unexplainable unimaginable mysteries make perfect sense, I UNDERSTAND, I feel it in five and more senses, I am with God, but I feel the moment — MOMENT! — seconds, my temporal life, slipping away and I'm on fire and I MUST ACT! *(Michael musters every bit of courage. To Betsy.)* Excuse me. *(Betsy smiles.)*

BETSY.   Sorry. *(Aside.)* I actually feel the emptiness between my legs.... I could just put my hands on his cheek, his neck, that tender skin. I could whisper, "Wanna come back to my place for some fun?" I could trace his bones with my fingers.... God, that strong but gentle thing unravels me, opens me, oh God, I could just hug him, I could just fuck him, I WANT TO GET LAID OR AT LEAST TOUCH A MAN.... Shit, he probably lives with his girlfriend, some beautiful bitch who keeps him on a leash and only lets him out to send on errands. Else he's heavy into S&M and wants to tie me up and spank me on the first date. I hate that shit on the first date — no mystery, no trust building, just some animal who wants to play the same game with every girl he meets. Actually, he looks insecure — more wimp than beast. Probably couldn't last long enough to satisfy me. Which is fine. Less stress. I have enough stress in my life, don't need to worry about squeezing some sweaty club inside me for hours on end just to pretend I'm not alone. Like he's really gonna notice me anyway. He probably doesn't even know he bumped into a female. I could be some east village punk with pierced testicles as far as he cares. I could be a gorilla escaped from the zoo. I could be the wall. Life is misery, missed opportunity — people, objects, ideas, subways, everything flying by too fast to net them in. And don't give me that, "They're all ranting!" The ones that can sip a drink alone, they're going: My keys! Where the fuck are my keys? Shit, I missed my train! What do you mean my electric's cut off? I sent the goddamn payment! That wall's too fucking high! I'm drowning in this shit! And nobody gives a flying fuck, step on my fucking head to keep their precious mouths a millimeter above the water line. Loss, loss, all is loss, loss, loss, loss, loss, ah fuck it, I'll be dead soon enough, a risk. A risk! I MUST ACT! *(Betsy turns to Michael.)* You like the show? *(Thunder.)*

MICHAEL.   *(Aside.)* Care, great care. I'm behind enemy lines. Snipers everywhere. Slightest misstep and it's over, I'm flesh on concrete. She blasted open the door and said okay, kid, whatcha got? Worthy of playing in my ballpark? My previous experience includes three little league games at Frankie Molenecki Field when I was nine, but suddenly I've received the call. The Yankees need me, and I'm in the stadium, it's the World Series, I've been brought in with loaded bases. I'm up by a run. Just one batter between me and a series championship and Babe Ruth is at the plate — he's back and playing for the Braves. Do I throw junk or just come in with the heat knowing the Babe hits heat better than anyone ever? Curve, I'll start with the curve. She'll probably just watch the first pitch anyway. She wants to see my stuff before SLAMMING IT! *(Beat.)* My god, I actually feel chemistry here and my mind is racing with clichés about baseball. But that's what I know. I never get women anyway. Maybe I need to think of it as more of a game ...

BETSY.   *(Exact repeat of above.)* You like the show?

MICHAEL.   You were terrific.

BETSY.   Why would you say that? *(Michael laughs.)*

MICHAEL.   *(Aside.)* Ball one, hung the curve but got away with it. Heat! Give her the heat. Just rare back and fire! Blow her down! *(To Betsy.)* Because ... I thought you were. I think I've seen you in the neighborhood before. You live around here?

BETSY.   *(Aside.)* Three good signs: One, he's talking to me. Two, he admitted that he might have noticed me before. Three, he brought up where I live as in where we might get naked and fuck.

MICHAEL.   *(As before.)* You live around here?

BETSY.   Block over, Sullivan and Spring.

MICHAEL.   *(Aside.)* Stee-ri-eek one! Painted the outside corner of the plate. I know where she lives and I'm standing not three hundred feet away right now. Alright, stick with the heat, it's working.... *(To Betsy.)* Easy commute to perform. *(She laughs. Aside.)* Stee-rike two!

BETSY.   *(Aside.)* Play it safe. Give him what he wants to hear ... *(To Michael.)* You're funny. *(Aside.)* Look at him smile. It's as if I said, "You have a beautiful penis, can I stroke it?"

MICHAEL.   I'm Michael. *(He holds out his hand. She takes it and they shake. Aside.)* We're touching. Contact. Warmth. So gentle.

BETSY. *(Aside.)* Sweaty palms.

MICHAEL. *(Aside.)* What a sweet little hand. What tenderness ...

BETSY. *(Aside.)* Fuck it, I'm on a roll. Pour it on thick. *(To Michael.)* I'm Betsy. I have a good feeling about meeting you. *(Band breaks into baseball tune, "Take Me Out To The Ballgame,"* as Michael goes through an elaborate umpire's call.)*

MICHAEL. *(Aside.)* Stee-rike three! You're outta there! It's over. The world series is mine! But don't get cocky. Nobody likes a gloater. Be gentlemanly yet interested. Give her a cheer. *(To Betsy.)* A good feeling? What kind of good feeling?

BETSY. *(Aside.)* The kind a woman gets when she feels she's met the man who'll hold her and make love to her the rest of her life, the man who will tell her she's pretty and good and important and all that other insecurity maintenance shit I say I don't need but so desperately long for and hate all my friends who seem to have it even though I act like their lives must be so boring and mine is so exciting because I'm free of all that picket fence, Polyanna, pass-the-margarine-please-fuckface bullshit. And the feeling of wanting just a nice, normal, sane guy and forgetting the sickening dating scene, the dinners and drinks with Henry the anal-retentive architect, Steven the moron and his family's electrical contracting bullshit boring business, Rob the sweet but ugly therapist with anal warts, Frank the stockbroker who thinks girls shouldn't work and laughs about it till he wheezes, Larry the lighting designer with his stubby fingers and eighteenth century chess set, Clarence who met me at Ellen's Stardust Diner for a drink and told me two minutes into our blind date to forget it 'cause he just wasn't attracted, no offense, and why waste good money on a bad vibe, and Winston who told me we should do it on the first date because all the bullshit of relationships boils down to compatibility in bed, and two Jewish lawyers named Barry, both annoyingly caught up in their litigious selves,

* See Special Note on Songs and Recordings on copyright page.

countless Davids and Johns and Peters and Alfred, my child-hood friend who takes me home, says he has something to show me, a videotape of his dead mother berating him to date me, him watching it glued to the screen, slurping ice cream on a TV tray, and a Swede named Gunter who asked me for money after I fucked him in a drunken desperate stupor on a manhunt evening with my compadre in love crime, Josie — Josie who got married last fall to Butch, a really sweet guy, and left me to rot alone!

MICHAEL. *(As before.)* A good feeling? What kind of good feeling?

BETSY. Maybe I shouldn't have said that.

MICHAEL. No, hell, why not? If you have a good feeling, you have a good feeling. And the truth is I have the same feeling or at least a fairly similar one. Funny how feelings work that way. *(Aside.)* That's so good. Should be writing this down.

BETSY. *(Aside, overlapping Michael's Aside.)* Gross, schmaltz, ooze, yuck! *(To Michael.)* Well, it's nice to meet you. Thanks for coming.

MICHAEL. We should get dinner sometime.

BETSY. *(Aside.)* Suddenly life turns in a moment. BAM! I'm in a situation. Hang in there. Tough it out. For God sakes, don't panic. *(To Michael.)* You don't play games....

MICHAEL. Why don't you give me your number and I'll ... *(Glorious loud music kicks in so that Betsy and Michael can no longer be heard. The music continues as they break into slow motion panto-mime: Betsy shrugs. Michael hands Betsy a scrap of paper. Betsy checks her pockets for a pen but can't find one. Michael pulls out a pen and gallantly offers it to Betsy. Betsy takes the pen and writes her number on the paper. She hands the paper back to Michael and puts the pen in her pocket. She then laughs and puts her hand to her mouth as if to say, "Oops." She takes the pen out of her pocket and hands it to Michael. He laughs and pockets the pen. Back to real time.)* So, we'll talk. I'll call you soon.

BETSY. Great. *(Lonnie walks over to them.)*

LONNIE. Hi guys.

BETSY. Hey. *(She hugs Lonnie.)*

MICHAEL. *(To Lonnie.)* Great stuff as usual, buddy. *(Michael hugs Lonnie.)*

LONNIE.   What do you expect?

BETSY.   You guys know each other?

MICHAEL.   If he wasn't my best friend, I'd be honest and tell him the evening sucked, but … *(Michael and Lonnie high five in slow motion as Betsy scowls.)*

BETSY.   *(Aside.)* There's something about men who know each other that bugs the hell out of me.

LONNIE.   *(To Betsy.)* I must have told you about Michael. He's my *male* monologue guy.

MICHAEL.   Which I guess inspired you to write for women.

LONNIE.   Yup. Gotta run kids. *(Beat.)* You guys should go out.

MICHAEL.   Master of tact … *(Lonnie starts off. He turns right into Josie who has just entered.)*

JOSIE.   Hello, Lonnie.

LONNIE.   "Hello" doesn't suit you, Josie. Just say hell. *(Josie hugs Betsy.)*

JOSIE.   Great job, sweetie. *(To Lonnie.)* Your wit is even more dazzling out of your own mouth. *(To Michael.)* I recognize you.

MICHAEL.   *(Pointing to Lonnie.)* Lonnie …

JOSIE.   Right. Hi.

BETSY.   *(Referring to Josie and Michael.)* Oh, so you guys …

JOSIE.   Yes, we guys …

LONNIE.   *(To Josie.)* Words can't express what a pleasure it is to see you, Jose.

JOSIE.   Ah, words …

LONNIE.   How's Butch?

JOSIE.   How sweet of you to know about me.

LONNIE.   I'm constantly asking Betsy for updates about the only true love of my life. Why do you think I cast her? *(Making a fast exit.)* Night kids!

BETSY.   Thanks, Lon! *(Lonnie exits.)*

MICHAEL.   *(To Betsy and Josie.)* Can I walk you out?

BETSY.   Sure. *(They exit. Betsy is in her apartment on the phone. Josie, elsewhere on stage, is in her apartment, phone in hand.)*

JOSIE.   Are you insane? I mean have you lost all perspective? That's impossible. It's not an option. Forget it. I mean, what's going on with you? Are you sick? Do you have a brain fever or something? Did you witness a murder? Did you get hit in the head? Did you o.d. on antihistamines? Talk to me Betsy. C'mon babe. It's like I don't even know you anymore. You're some stranger.

BETSY.   I just want to fucking call him. It's been a week already. What's the goddamn problem?

JOSIE.   I'm speechless. No comment.

BETSY.   What!?

JOSIE.   No, no, I've read about this. You can't help friends this far gone. You think you can, you delude yourself into thinking you can stop them, but the reality is you can only be there at the end to tell 'em you love and care about 'em and say nice things at the funeral.

BETSY.   Okay, Jose, I get the point.

JOSIE.   I don't know that you do. A woman calling a guy in this kinda scenario — when he said he'd call you and didn't even give you his number — is like saying, "Hey, how you doing? I'm a desperate loser who hasn't been loved in years and probably never will be because I'm pathetic and everybody knows." *(Beat.)* You *sure* Lonnie didn't say anything?

BETSY.   Lonnie didn't say shit. Played stupid.

JOSIE.   Lonnie loves fucking with minds. It's his hobby, sends his resume to fascist governments looking for internships. Think hard, Bets. He must've given some indication that he was concealing something. Guys get extremely self-conscious when they conceal, try too hard to cover. Even Lonnie. You know, like he *paused* when you asked him some simple question. Like you — okay, okay — you were talking about the play — alright? — and his *response* didn't quite jibe with the issue at hand, like, for instance, you asked him how he felt about the piece — okay? — and rather than just saying like straight out, boom, "Oh, yeah, I thought you did a great job, but you need to turn out more during the fight scene," and whatever the fuck else he'd say, he said, "Uh, uh, oh, yeah yeah yeah! uh, I thought it was ... great." You see what I'm getting at? Like he was *distracted*, hiding something, like he had a secret.

BETSY. Nah, he didn't flinch.

JOSIE. *(With admiration.)* He's good, a master. Not tipping his hand ...

BETSY. What hand? We're not talking about limbs and digits. We're dealing with a voice, vocal resonance over a goddamn phone line. Fucking Michael doesn't have to get physical, except for lifting the receiver.

JOSIE. He could be afraid you changed your mind. Maybe he's intimidated by you. Thinks you might bag on him. Maybe his last girlfriend fucked him over so bad he ain't gonna get in with another girl for twenty years. Maybe she fell asleep while they were fucking. Maybe she made fun of his dick. Maybe she *had* a dick. Hell, maybe he's dead.

BETSY. You're really cheering me up.

JOSIE. What? How do we know the guy's not dead? This is New York City. He could've been hit by a taxi right after you met him. Boom. End of romance.

BETSY. I think Lonnie would've mentioned that.

JOSIE. Well ... maybe there was some tragedy in his family — his brother didn't get into Harvard ... his father was insulted at a cocktail party ... his mother's facelift is too tight and she can't close her eyes ... maybe he had an emergency tonsillectomy and can't talk ... maybe he was kidnapped ... maybe he hit his head and got amnesia and forgot you existed. WE DON'T KNOW. It's all a crap shoot at this point. Speculation. Like the stock market, horse races, but we have no insider line. All we have is patience and the superhuman ability to not even think of calling him. Hell, we're chattin' this guy up so much and he could be Charlie Manson's demented cousin for all we know. We're dealing with Lonnie Goldman's best friend. Could be some freak-whacko-crack dealer-pimp-terrorist. We need more information and it ain't coming from Lonnie. I mean, I guess I'm saying ... I don't know what I'm saying ... but NONE OF THIS MEANS HE WON'T CALL. That's as much of a mystery as ... as life-after-death, the threat of alien invasion ... hell, IT'S AS MUCH OF A MYSTERY AS THE FEMALE DESIRE TO BE WITH THESE BASTARDS NO MATTER HOW MUCH THEY REINFORCE

WHAT TOTAL SHITS THEY ARE ON EVERY POSSIBLE LEVEL. Hang in there babe.

BETSY. Ah, he's not gonna call. A week already. Fuckin' guy. I mean I don't understand the logic — guys say they're gonna call then they don't. If he so didn't want to call then he shouldn't have said he fucking would. It's not like I put a bazooka to his groin and said, "Take my number and tell me you're going to call me or I'll blow your fuckin' balls off." It's just a little human compassion I'm looking for here. Maybe that's a lot to ask for nowadays, I don't know. I just don't think one should treat language and communication so fucking flippantly. It's all we have to go on. Communication, right? — language being the primary carrier of communication between humans. Sets us apart from other life forms, right? If you're not gonna call, don't say you're gonna fuckin' call. What, is it some male-power-trip-mind-fuck-sick-asshole shit to tell someone he's calling and then *not* call? Not calling. Should be a criminal offense. Guys wouldn't pull it anymore if they knew they'd be doing hard time. It's all bullshit. Talk. Language. Meaningless bullshit. Ah, fuck him. FUCK HIM. Wouldn't go out with the bastard even if he did have the goddamn fuckin' audacity to call. Jesus, why are we even wasting our time on this fuck? I don't even know if I really liked him. It was just stupid overwhelming sexual attraction. He's probably totally insecure. He shuffled a little bit while we were talking. And his hair was definitely questionable.

JOSIE. What, is he balding?

BETSY. Nah, it's just too nice, like he's some fucking hair club guy. He probably blow dries it and uses gel and is self-conscious about it while fucking. It wouldn't have worked out. *(A loud tone is heard. It's call waiting.)* Oh hell, could you hold on a sec?

JOSIE. Sure, but hurry up. I gotta yell at Butch.

BETSY. Thanks. *(She clicks her phone.)* Yeah? Hi. Uh … uh … oh yeah, yeah, of course, h … h … yeah hold one sec … *(Clicks phone again.)* It's him!

JOSIE. You gonna talk?

BETSY. Yeah. Any final words of wisdom?

JOSIE.   Use contraception. *(Betsy laughs hysterically.)*
BETSY.   Bye. *(She clicks phone again.)* Sorry! *(Lights cut out on Betsy and Josie. Lights up on Michael's apartment. We go back in time. Michael holds a phone in his hand and starts dialing. Lonnie is watching a baseball game on TV and holding a football.)*
LONNIE.   Wait! *(Michael slams down the phone.)*
MICHAEL.   I don't understand. Why shouldn't I call if I know I like her and she seemed to like me?
LONNIE.   You have fucked up every prospect you've had in the last seven years because you're too eager. You meet a woman, you call her the next day. That's eager, and it's a turn off. EAGER IS UGLY. It's even an ugly word. Ee-geur! Women hate that shit. They want a little mystery. Because down deep they hate themselves. That's why they desperately want to be able to say, "Who the fuck is this arrogant asshole? What's his story? That fucker thinks he can tell me he's gonna call and then not call?" Now you'll never meet a woman who'll admit to actually being turned on by this. They all say, "I don't play games. Some people do, but I'm different." Everybody claims to be different, but it's bullshit. They're all the same — love a guy who treats 'em like shit. AT FIRST. Once things get rolling, you're on your own, and you're subject to a whole other slew of mystery and emotion and hormonally induced nightmares that's too complicated to even think about on any level of conscious thought. But *your* problem is you're too nice at the *beginning* and you don't get anything going. *That's* why I'm here. Think of this as a complimentary service to my best buddy who I'd love to see get laid so I don't have to listen anymore about how you never get laid. Michael, you're a goddamn headcase about that shit. I'm not letting you fuck this one up because I want to be able to rest easy knowing you're getting laid.
MICHAEL.   I've already waited a week. I wanted to call her the next day. Hell, I wanted to call her that night. But I listened to your bullshit and now it's been a goddamn week.
LONNIE.   Wait a month.
MICHAEL.   Lonnie, I told her I'd call.
LONNIE.   Did you tell her when? *(Michael throws up his arms.)*

There you go.

MICHAEL. But she'll be pissed. *(Lonnie, exasperated, picks up the remote control and turns off the TV. He passes the football to Michael. They continue to pass the football back and forth across the apartment during Lonnie's speech.)*

LONNIE. Are you listening to anything I'm saying? Of course she'll be pissed. That doesn't make it a negative. Fallacy number one. Sure, she's upset, she's cursing you, wishes you were dead. BUT YOU'RE ON HER MIND. If we're lucky, she may even have cried herself to sleep over it. Maybe she's distracted at work. She's embarrassed because she told all her friends about you and they keep asking her if you called. You know, stickin' in the blade ... great, great, great! The more she's pissed, the better. That's PASSION. Before, you were just another guy. Now, your stock has gone up. All the other loser nice guy idiots call the next day, just like they call their mommies when they're supposed to. Boooooooorring! The point is, if she likes you, you could call her five years from now and she'll still go out with you. Waiting to call can only help. It can't hurt. I've never heard of a case where a guy didn't call and got turned down.

MICHAEL. I think this case is different. We really had a spark ...

LONNIE. Everyone thinks his case is different. Fallacy number two. Everyone's the same. These mating rituals pre-date humanity. Do you know how moose get together?

MICHAEL. I take it they don't call each other.

LONNIE. The male moose comes up behind the female and taps his hoof ever so gently against her back leg, barely even making contact. She runs away, of course. Doesn't want some big hairy fuckin' moose all over her. No problem for the male moose. He's cool. He's calm. He ain't rushing anything. He knows the deal with these female moose. He waits a bit, then he nonchalantly saunters behind her and taps again ... gently. Again, she skidaddles. She ain't that kinda girl. Not gonna jump in the sack with this guy so fast.

MICHAEL. I'm not talking about jumping in the sack ...

LONNIE. Now, most of the time, she's gonna keep running

and he'll get the point that she's not gonna do the nasty with him no matter how many times or how sensually he taps, and that'll be that. Doesn't matter if he's the biggest moose stud there ever was. BUT, sometimes, and again it's the exception, eventually, after they go through this tapping stuff several times, she'll start to think he's kinda cute, they'll flirt, then she'll get all turned on and she'll stretch herself into the moose mating position and, well, the rest is too disgusting to even mention, doesn't matter. The point is, the male taps, TAPS ever so gently. He's patient. If he taps too hard, she flees and that's that. He'll never see her again.

MICHAEL.   I have absolutely no idea how moose sex relates to whether or not I should call this woman.

LONNIE.   It's the same thing! She's the moose! You bash her over the head, she's gonna bolt. You gotta tap.

MICHAEL.   You saying calling is bashing her over the head?

LONNIE.   Exactly.

MICHAEL.   How else am I supposed to make contact? Smoke signals?

LONNIE.   You gotta be patient. Didn't your parents ever teach you patience is a virtue?

MICHAEL.   It doesn't feel right.

LONNIE.   She's a fawn at a pond sipping water.

MICHAEL.   Thirty seconds ago she was a self-hating bitch, then a moose, now she's Bambi's sister.

LONNIE.   But one quick movement and she'll prance off so quickly, you won't even be sure she was ever there. You got a big marlin on the line. You have to reel it in nice and slow. You can't shake the worm.

MICHAEL.   Lonnie ...

LONNIE.   Yeah, buddy?

MICHAEL.   Get the fuck out of my apartment.

LONNIE.   You're not gonna do anything rash...?

MICHAEL.   Out!

LONNIE.   You pick up that phone, you're in the middle of the jungle on your own. And I don't want to hear about it.

MICHAEL.   Yeah, full of moose and fawns and fish, I'll take my chances.

LONNIE.   There are bears in the forest, beasts in the jungle. Anything could happen. You can't go in alone. I am offering to be your guide, your Sherpa, to take your hand and lead you through the darkness. *(Michael pushes him toward the door.)*

MICHAEL.   I have my Swiss army knife. I'll be fine.

LONNIE.   *(Exiting.)* No sudden movements, tap … gently! *(Lonnie is gone. Michael pulls out the scrap of paper with the phone number. He picks up the phone, takes a deep breath and dials. Lights come up on Betsy's area. Betsy plays this mini-scene exactly as before. This time, we hear and see Michael as well. We do <u>not</u> hear and see Josie. A loud tone is heard.)*

BETSY.   *(On phone.)* Oh hell, could you hold on a sec? Thanks. *(She clicks her phone.)* Yeah …

MICHAEL.   Hey Betsy, it's Michael … from Lonnie's show last week …

BETSY.   Hi.

MICHAEL.   You remember me?

BETSY.   Uh … uh … oh yeah, yeah, of course.

MICHAEL.   I just thought …

BETSY.   H-

MICHAEL.   … maybe we could …

BETSY.   H-

MICHAEL.   … get together if …

BETSY.   Yeah, hold one sec …

MICHAEL.   Oh, sure … *(Betsy clicks phone again.)*

BETSY.   It's him! *(Pause.)* Yeah. Any final words of wisdom?

MICHAEL.   *(Aside, overlapping Betsy's previous line and the next one.)* How could I not realize she had call waiting? Jesus, I'm trying to ask her out and she's trying to get rid of me. TAP! My God, I just nailed her in the head with a sledgehammer. *(Betsy laughs hysterically.)*

BETSY.   Bye. *(She clicks phone again.)* Sorry!

MICHAEL.   I didn't realize you had call waiting.

BETSY.   Yeah. *(During the following, Betsy attempts to interject a few times, when Michael takes breaths, only to be cut off again and again by his verbal barrage.)*

MICHAEL.   I don't have it 'cause to me it's like an intrusion, it changes the rules of the game, talking on the phone

I mean, it depersonalizes it a bit, no offense, but it's like you have to choose who you're going to talk to, who you like more, and I'm flattered you chose me, but it's just like all technology, the question is: Does it really benefit man, I mean *people*, sorry, or does it just make us crazier? Like if there was no overnight mail, then you wouldn't have to worry about people getting stuff out faster than you ... *(Michael continues while Betsy:)*

BETSY. *(Aside.)* This guy'd be so much cuter if he'd just shut the fuck up. I'm being bombarded, pelted by his words. Every word less attractive than the last. Words words words, language. Junk language, like fumes that float into the ether and makes us all insane. Putrid, dilapidated words, like garbage — festering nouns, rotten adjectives, decrepit verbs with crutches and walkers barely able to make it off his tongue. These insecure men with their atrocities of language. You can't dump garbage illegally, but you can litter the air freely. I should just hang up now, cut my losses.

MICHAEL. *(Softly overlapping Betsy's Aside as he rushes through his words.)* ... Everyone would have to wait a week for delivery of important documents, or whatever. I mean, however long it took, it would take and, well, I'm not saying I don't appreciate overnight mail or call waiting or any technology. I'm spoiled like everyone else, but if we never had it, we wouldn't know what we were missing. I mean, I'm glad I got through to you, but I choose not to have call waiting because I don't want to be interrupted when I'm on the phone. My friends get through eventually and always complain, so for me it's really more of a statement against the technology which ultimately, I think, doesn't make the world a better place. I mean, is the economy better? Look at computers, for instance. *(Betsy finishes her Aside.)* If there were no computers, then businesses wouldn't have to worry that other businesses had employees that could do the work of ten, and more people would be employed, quite possibly. It's complicated because there might be fewer businesses in that scenario. It's a subtle point but something I've thought about a lot. *(Long pause. Betsy is speechless. Michael awaits her response.)*

23

BETSY. Wow. I never thought of it that way. It's ... fascinating.

MICHAEL. *(Aside.)* Yes! And fucking Lonnie said don't call! The moose, the fawn and the marlin are crowded around, entranced. *(To Betsy, into phone.)* Ah, it's boring, just my little pet theory.

BETSY. *(Aside.)* Better give him a little bit of a hard time so he knows he can't pull shit with me.... *(To Michael, into phone.)* So I didn't think you'd call ...

MICHAEL. What!?

BETSY. I mean you said you'd call ... but you didn't ...

MICHAEL. It's been, work, helluva week, lots of deadlines, you know newspapers ...

BETSY. Not really ...

MICHAEL. Editors want copy. I was workin' all night, I would've called, wanted to, but ...

BETSY. I'll let you redeem yourself.

MICHAEL. Dinner?

BETSY. Break bread, huh?

MICHAEL. As ancient a ritual as breaking heads.... *(Aside.)* Oops!

BETSY. *(Aside.)* Psycho?

MICHAEL. *(Desperately covering.)* I ... I mean like war. Mankind, people kind, been making war as long as we've been making food and, well, I prefer food. I make food. How 'bout I make you dinner?

BETSY. *(Aside.)* His bullshit is sorta kinda cute in a nauseating way ... most likely harmless. *(To Michael, into phone.)* I prefer neutral ground ... for a first date ...

MICHAEL. Of course. What's your favorite restaurant?

BETSY. Dangerous question. *(Aside.)* Please God, don't let him say "Danger's my middle name."

MICHAEL. *(Aside, simultaneously with Betsy.)* Danger's my middle name...? *(He's about to say it then reconsiders. Aside.)* ... nah. A cliché and it's dorky. Remain cool. What's the cool response?

BETSY. *(As before.)* Dangerous question.

MICHAEL. I'm willing to take a risk with you.

BETSY. *(Aside.)* That's good. *(To Michael, into phone.)* If you insist, Union Square Cafe.

MICHAEL. *(Aside.)* Yup. That's expensive. *(To Betsy, into phone.)* I love it. Saturday night?

BETSY. *(Aside.)* Weekend night. I'm impressed. Man of substance. *(To Michael, into phone.)* What do you know? It's my only free night the next eight months.

MICHAEL. Tremendous luck. You still have a good feeling?

BETSY. Well, the feeling has ... evolved, shall we say ...

MICHAEL. Evolution is good ...

BETSY. Been good to me ... just gotta watch out for revolution and dissolution.

MICHAEL. Well, as they say, I know where you live.

BETSY. Oh my.

MICHAEL. Exact address?

BETSY. 203 Spring, number 5.

MICHAEL. Eight o'clock?

BETSY. How prime!

MICHAEL. I look forward to it.

BETSY. I bet you do.

MICHAEL. You free now?

BETSY. Goodnight, Michael.

MICHAEL. It is, Betsy. Sleep tight. *(She hangs up. Michael stares at his receiver then hangs up.)*

MICHAEL and BETSY. *(Aside.)* The most flirtatious phone conversation I've had in years. Definitely a vibe.

MICHAEL. *(To Betsy.)* You think so?

BETSY. I said it, didn't I?

MICHAEL. I mean it was like our thoughts were moving into the real conversation.

BETSY. That's a vibe, right?

MICHAEL. Can we kiss in our thoughts?

BETSY. We could do whatever we want. It's just imagination. We could fuck each other like wild moose all night ...

MICHAEL. Excuse me?

BETSY. We could do whatever we want, you don't know that?

MICHAEL. Why moose? Most people say dogs or rabbits when using that cliché.

BETSY. Oh, moose are much more passionate.

MICHAEL. Really?

BETSY. They're more discriminating than other animals. They only do it if it truly feels right. Pretty sophisticated sexually.

MICHAEL. Amazing.

BETSY. I'll take a moose over a dog or rabbit any day. Most men are dogs or rabbits or some disgusting combination of the two.

MICHAEL. Am I a moose?

BETSY. I don't know yet. Hope so.

MICHAEL. Me too.

BETSY. Well, sweet dreams. *(She starts to go.)*

MICHAEL. Isn't that what this is?

BETSY. In a way.

MICHAEL. So why don't we ... you know ... like moose ...

BETSY. You're not the only thing on my mind. Is that what you men think? I got other stuff to consider. Ya know, like my whole life.

MICHAEL. Oh.

BETSY. *Ciao! (She leaves.)*

MICHAEL. I can't think of anything else to think about. I can't think, period. *(Michael leaves. Betsy and Michael return and play out the Narrator's speech through movement.)*

NARRATOR. Three days pass during which they each take the time to consider what they'll wear then make sure it will be clean the night of the date. Michael hasn't been to the dentist in a while so he goes in for a checkup and gets his teeth cleaned. Betsy gets her legs and bikini line waxed even though she doesn't plan to go far enough for it to really matter. It is a precaution, just in case. She also sets aside her best underwear. Michael, in the meantime, agonizes over whether or not he should get a haircut and decides not to because it would be too much of a risk. Betsy briefly considers a hair maneuver, something a little sexier, wispier, perhaps, but holds off. Michael learns that getting a reservation at Union Square Cafe is not easy. They are booked several weeks in advance for Saturday nights. He goes to the restaurant in person on Thursday and is actually able to get a reservation for nine o'clock with a hundred dollar bribe to Richard, the ever-smiling manager of the popular establishment. Michael is quite pleased with himself for this. He wouldn't have been as pleased if he had known that Richard would have taken fifty. At three o'clock on the day of the date, Michael takes a jog, something he hasn't done in several weeks, but he heard exercise reduces stress and he is feeling a bit stressed out over the big night. While Michael is jogging, Betsy preps. She takes a bubble bath and applies a green clay facial mask to clean out her pores. Michael returns from the jog and flips on the Yankee game. *(We hear the sound of a baseball broadcast in the background.)*

BASEBALL ANNOUNCER.   *(V.O.)* ... beautiful day here at Yankee Stadium.

NARRATOR.   Every time any player gets a base hit, Michael does thirty push-ups. It is a high-scoring game and he tortures himself to bulk up for the evening.

BASEBALL ANNOUNCER.   *(V.O.)* ... haven't seen this much offense in a single game in years ...

NARRATOR.   Betsy applies cucumber and tea bags to her eyes to reduce puffiness. Just before eight o'clock, she slaps her face several times, hangs her head upside down, and bites her lip to get color. *(Betsy's apartment. Betsy is maniacally rushing to get ready. Michael appears at door and rings doorbell.)*

BETSY.   Fuck! *(She checks her watch.)* On time. What is it with this fuckin' guy? *(Shouts.)* Coming! *(Michael fidgets.)*

MICHAEL.   *(To himself.)* Cool. Remain calm. Be cautious. No wild shots. Play a control game. Half court defense. Be patient. Pass the ball, fergodsakes. Wait for a good shot. *(Betsy opens the door.)*

BETSY.   Hey, come on in.

MICHAEL.   Hey! How you doin'?

BETSY.   *(Rushing.)* Good, great, fine. Have a chair, I'll be with you in a sec assuming I don't choke on this fucking bra.

MICHAEL.   No problem. Take your time. It's great to see you. *(Michael goes to sit. Betsy retreats to her bedroom, offstage. We hear her as she continues readying herself.)*

BETSY.   *(Offstage.)* That's sweet. Women probably tell you you're sweet, right?

MICHAEL. Uh, my mother thinks so ... *(Pause.)*
BETSY. *(Offstage.)* I'm gonna be honest with you. I don't like mother references. Boys and their mommies worry me.
MICHAEL. Okay ...
BETSY. *(Offstage.)* No offense. Really. You are sweet. It's your thing, your routine. Not that it's phony or anything. It's just like your shtick, your rap, demeanor. You're a sweetie. It's a good thing, don't worry about it.
MICHAEL. Thanks. *(Aside.)* She's a little weird, but I am a thousand percent attracted to that pretty face, intense little body and lips and legs and breasts and cute tight little butt.
BETSY. *(Aside, popping her head back on stage.)* He's a little wimpy, but what a cutey — pretty face, nice body, great eyes, and cute tight little butt.
MICHAEL. *(Aside.)* It's amazing how many women I meet who I feel nothing toward and then BOOM, I'm sitting in the apartment of a goddess. Her pheromones are intense! *(Betsy bursts back into the room.)*
BETSY. Ready!
NARRATOR. What follows are selected shorts from dinner at Union Square Cafe. Through the miracle of slide projection, we will see into their minds and read their exact thoughts. *(Betsy and Michael sit at a table. Behind them is a screen. As they talk, their thoughts are projected above them onto the screen. The sequence is a series of short scenes. Each new scene is punctuated by a shift in bodily attitude and a change of background piano bar music.)*

Scene 1

MICHAEL'S SCREEN: She's impressed. Women love this family stuff.
BETSY'S SCREEN: Why is he telling me this?

MICHAEL. ... so then my sister got a nose job and of course she looked like she got hit by a truck and my brother and I

made fun of her, I mean we were kids, and my mother ...
BETSY. *(Overlapping.)* Uh-huh, uh-huh, uh-huh ...

Scene 2

MICHAEL'S SCREEN: God, she's beautiful.
BETSY'S SCREEN: Am I attracted to him?

BETSY.   ... I don't know if I'm gonna act anymore. They
keep giving me more and more writing at the agency. That's
how I pay my bills. I'm a copywriter. I actually enjoy it a lot
of the time.
MICHAEL.   That's great. I mean I write for the Press, one
of the free papers, and I hate it. You're lucky.

Scene 3

MICHAEL'S SCREEN: I'm in love. [# drinks consumed: 1
1/2]
BETSY'S SCREEN: He's such a cutey. [# drinks consumed: 1]

MICHAEL.   ... I just don't need to manufacture excitement.
There's enough in human relationships and art. Like parachut-
ing. I have no interest. I don't need to jump out of a plane
to get a rush. I'd rather sit and read the newspaper with someone I care about and talk about what really matters ...
BETSY.   Like what?

Scene 4

MICHAEL'S SCREEN: Don't say anything stupid. Just listen
and nod. [# drinks consumed: 2 1/2]

BETSY'S SCREEN: He's definitely hot when he shuts up. [# drinks consumed: 2]

BETSY. ... It boils down to this. Men are sensitive about their hair, women are sensitive about their breasts. *(Michael nods. His screen changes. Letters fill the screen:)*

MICHAEL'S SCREEN: BREASTS
(Michael reaches and takes Betsy's hand. A big moment.)
MICHAEL'S SCREEN: Warm nice oh oh mmmmm !XO! ooooh aaaah ...
BETSY'S SCREEN: Do I take him home or not?

Scene 5

BETSY'S SCREEN: Shit, I drank too much. [# drinks consumed: 4]
MICHAEL'S SCREEN: Wonder what she looks like naked? [# drinks consumed: 5]

BETSY. ... and Lloyd was a jerk from London, wanted a green card. Only lasted seven or so months. And Joe! A month in Prague in between jobs to draw. My instructor, taught me to do perspective. We visited his family in this little Bohemian town with a population of like nine. Mother didn't approve of me, something to do with some European shit. Then there was Larry. Thirty-year-old lighting designer. Said he was a virgin — left him that way after a couple weeks. And here we are!
MICHAEL. Wow, it's like the history channel. I think someone should document this stuff. Why do you have to be famous to have your life recorded? I think *your* life is a helluva lot more interesting than ... Eli Whitney's — you are so beautiful....

Scene 6

BETSY'S SCREEN: Please let's get outta here. [# drinks consumed: 4]
MICHAEL'S SCREEN: Wonder what she looks like naked? [# drinks consumed: 5 1/2]

MICHAEL. ... I just think life is the ultimate interactive game. Like now. Imagine if this was an interactive game where you could talk to another person and hold hands and have feelings toward them. Wouldn't that be incredible? But it could never be as incredible as the real thing, which is this, now. Life itself really is this elaborate game with a definite beginning and end. And the end really is the end. What's in between ... well, some play better than others, some have more luck than others ... when you really think about it, it's like you're just watching and making moves. You have relationships, your job, your entertainment, your stress, the whole package which is life. I watch what's going on around me, like it's TV but it's this huge amazing 3-D screen surrounding me on all sides. I'm in the screen and I could affect what's going on and I could be affected by it all. All these computer people are coming up with these interactive games, these virtual reality games, and they'll never top the ultimate interactive game which is our lives, which is our constant reality, which is far more breathtaking than any imitation can ever be. Take you, for instance, sitting across from me ... beautiful, inspiring, transcendent.
BETSY. Me? This must be one of those games. You wanna get outta here?
MICHAEL. *(Raising arm.)* Check please! *(Michael and Betsy leave the restaurant. Michael bravely takes Betsy's hand as they stroll through the night. They arrive at Betsy's door.)* I had such a great night.
BETSY. Me too.

MICHAEL. Yeah. *(Series of quick movements under the microscope: Licking lips, head tilts, weight shifting from one side to other, glancing at one another's lips, ever-so-slightly biting lips, looking down at floor, deep breaths, nods, fingers rubbing side, smiles.)* Well, g'night. *(They kiss. As they kiss:)*

LONNIE. If you call her, she'll know you like her. *(They break the kiss.)*

MICHAEL. *(Confused.)* Yeah...? *(Betsy goes into her apartment. Split stage: Michael and Lonnie in Michael's apartment. Betsy and Josie in Betsy's. Lonnie plays a video game.)*

LONNIE. That's the worst thing that could happen. May as well forget the whole thing, move on.

MICHAEL. Didn't kissing her indicate that I like her?

LONNIE. How?

MICHAEL. We kissed. It was nice.

LONNIE. Yeah...?

MICHAEL. I told her I had a nice time.

LONNIE. I'm not following your line of reasoning here. Haven't you ever fucked a girl you hated? *(Michael is about to respond:)* Forget it, you're a bad example. You're like some aberrant freak. Believe me, I've kissed women I wished were never born. Fuckin' around, messin' around and *liking* someone are two totally different things. *(At Betsy's place, Josie and Betsy sit in yoga positions on the floor. They breathe in, hold for a moment.)*

JOSIE. ... and exhale! *(Betsy exhales.)* And as you do, all thoughts of men are leaving your system. You are purged, clean, disinfected. *(Betsy falls over on her side and bangs the floor.)*

BETSY. Aaaah, I want to talk to him! *(Beat.)*

JOSIE. Okay, so that didn't work.

BETSY. Shit, Jose, it's the same crap all over again. Why can't I just call him? I'm a feminist.

JOSIE. Hey, don't abuse the "f" word. Feminism is great — we can vote, fight in wars, breast-feed in restaurants — but it's done little for relationships. If anything, it's complicated things because we say there shouldn't be a double standard anymore, but there is and always will be.

BETSY. You just called Butch.

JOSIE. We're married.

BETSY. So?

JOSIE. You call him, he'll *know* you like him. That's the worst ... *(The two scenes blend. Lonnie prepares a bong.)*

LONNIE. Okay. Okay. You engaged the enemy. It was an impassioned battle. You fought valiantly. You won the battle. But this is a war. Don't get excited. You gotta think. This is the time for cold, hard logic. Calculation. You've got troops out there. They're your responsibility, man. They have families. One bad phone call, *(He lights a match and inhales deeply from the bong.)* it's a blood bath.

JOSIE. Okay. Okay. Let's look at the facts. First date. Saturday night. Kissed. Textbook response is he calls Wednesday night at 9:30. We can measure his level of interest based on how much before or after that he calls. Problem is ...

LONNIE. DO *NOT* CALL HER.

JOSIE. ... aggravating circumstances.

LONNIE. I repeat: Do not call.

BETSY and MICHAEL. Haven't we already been through this?

LONNIE. Yes! And thank God you waited a week the first time.

JOSIE. Thank God you didn't call him the first time. Don't make the same potential mistake you almost potentially made the first time.

BETSY and MICHAEL. Huh?

MICHAEL. We had a great date. Why can't we just stop playing games?

JOSIE. Let me ask you a question.

BETSY. What?

LONNIE. Do you want this thing to work out?

BETSY and MICHAEL. Look, I just ...

JOSIE and LONNIE. No, no, just answer the question.

JOSIE. Do you want this guy to fall for you?

MICHAEL. Of course.

JOSIE. Then buck up. You're acting like a teenager.

LONNIE. You ever hear of a guy named Niccolo Machiavelli? He had a little saying ...

JOSIE. You do whatever the fuck it takes to get whatever the fuck you want. Period. Cut the Miss I'm-for-real-I-don't-play-games-I'm-a-liberated-woman bullshit.

LONNIE. Cut the Mister I'm-a-sensitive-guy-I-want-to-act-on-my-romantic-instincts garbage. It's goddamn nauseating to hear that slop, gives me gastronomic trouble. I'm serious, it does.

BETSY. But there was something about him, about us.

MICHAEL. I can't explain it.

JOSIE. Then call.

LONNIE. Go ahead. *(Michael and Betsy are about to speak.)*

JOSIE and LONNIE. No, no, just call.

JOSIE. But if you want something special, something lasting and beautiful ...

LONNIE. If you want her to hump the ground after you walk on it ...

JOSIE and LONNIE. ... PLAY THE GAME! *(Lonnie and Josie scram. Michael and Betsy play out the Narrator's speech.)*

NARRATOR. Confounded, Michael and Betsy refrain from calling for yet another week. Michael finally calls Betsy, and they make plans to meet two days later and see *Casablanca* at the Anthology. They have a great time. The most wonderful moment of the evening for Betsy is when Michael impulsively leans over and kisses her on the cheek during a romantic scene. For Michael, the most special moment comes just before he kisses Betsy goodnight and says what's on his mind ... *(At Betsy's door.)*

BETSY. Here we are again ...

MICHAEL. Listen, I really like you, okay? I don't want to play games. I want to see you again soon. How's that sound?

BETSY. Sounds just fine. *(They kiss. Music kicks in.)*

NARRATOR. Two weeks pass during which they, as Michael suggested, do not play games. They simply enjoy one another, grateful to be in a relationship, happy to be a couple and to have each other, though they do not make love. They both know that sex will happen when the moment is right, physically *and* emotionally. They sense things are getting a tad serious when Betsy invites Michael for a jogging date ... *(They jog. Betsy is clearly in better shape than Michael. Michael struggles to keep up.)*

MICHAEL. *(Aside.)* God, I really want this to work. I don't want her to think I'm an out-of-shape piece of shit.

BETSY. *(Aside.)* God, I really want this to work. I don't want him to think I think he's an out-of-shape piece of shit.

MICHAEL. How you doing?

BETSY. Fine. You want to rest?

MICHAEL. Only if you do.

BETSY. Either way is fine with me.

MICHAEL. I'm fine. Race you to that pole!

BETSY. Okay … *(They sprint for a moment then continue in slow motion. Still in slow motion, Michael stumbles and falls dramatically.)*

MICHAEL. *(Aside, as he falls.)* Oh shit. I'm an idiot, a klutz. What a fuckin' spaz. I can't believe this is happening. She'll think I'm a total loser. I blew it. I finally meet a woman I like and I fuck it up. *(Return to real time motion. Michael has sprained his ankle and winces in pain. Betsy stands over him.)*

BETSY. You okay? *(Michael springs to his feet. He lifts his left ankle, clearly in pain.)*

MICHAEL. I'm fine. *(He tries to walk, but the ankle hurts too much. Betsy helps him.)*

BETSY. C'mon, I'll take you home. *(Betsy hails a cab.)* Taxi! *(A cab pulls over — three chairs will do. They get in. The Cabby, a foreigner who barely speaks English, is particularly happy and effusive.)*

CABBY. Hi, how are you?

BETSY. West 3rd and Sullivan.

CABBY. Thank you! *(Cab pulls away.)*

BETSY. How's it feel?

MICHAEL. Bad. *(Betsy tenderly touches the wounded limb.)*

BETSY. We'll make it better. *(Cabby drives like a maniac, making sharp turns, speeding over pot holes. Michael squeals in pain as they bounce around. To Cabby.)* Hey, we want to get there alive, okay?

CABBY. Bad streets.

BETSY. No, bad driver. Slow down. *(Cabby speeds on.)*

CABBY. New York. Tense driving. Sorry. *(Michael grabs his ankle in pain.)*

BETSY. No, not sorry, slow the fuck down.

CABBY. Be there soon!

BETSY. Alright, fuckhead, pull over. *(Cabby smiles and nods.)*

CABBY. Be there soon!

MICHAEL. *(To Betsy.)* It's okay.

BETSY. No, it's not. *(To Cabby.)* Listen, you slow the fuck down and let us out or I'll make sure you never drive a moving vehicle ever again in your life. You won't be legal to ride your kid's tricycle.

MICHAEL. *(To Betsy.)* It's okay!

BETSY. *(To Michael.)* You're injured. Keep out of this.

CABBY. Thank you! *(The Cabby slams on the brakes. They have arrived.)* Five fifty.

BETSY. Shouldn't pay.

MICHAEL. I really think ... *(Michael digs into his pocket.)*

BETSY. Fine, fine. *(Betsy pays Cabby.)* You're lucky I'm paying you.

CABBY. Thank you! *(Betsy helps Michael out of the cab. Cabby scoots.)*

NARRATOR. That night is special for Michael and Betsy. Due to Michael's sprained ankle, they decide not to go out. Instead, they sit in Michael's apartment and read. *(Choreographed romantic scene with music of Michael and Betsy reading together.)* As they read, they realize something is happening inside them and in the room, as if the floor has disappeared and they are floating. They feel a powerful urge to hold one another ... *(They stop reading and kiss. Choreographed scene of Michael and Betsy making love for the first time. Michael's Dream Ballet and beyond. Choreographed movement and music accompanies Narrator.)* Later, as they sleep together in Michael's bed, Michael dreams of their entire relationship, from now until death — a full life together starting with this night then marriage vows and a kiss then children, mortgages, car loans, breakfasts in bed, family vacations, some fights, lovemaking, the kids go off to school, little Jodie joins a cult but they hire someone to get her out and then she's fine and she marries Henry, the investment banker with the big mole on his right cheek which fourteen years later turns into melanoma and he dies, leaving their grandchildren fatherless so they spend more time with Jodie and Ingrid and Horatio, the smart one, their little genius who does everything so well and that date rape thing was just a horrible accusation and HORIE COMES OUT ON TOP and they dance at S.O.B.'s during their second honeymoon forty years later and turn up the flame on their still-fiery romance and death comes from cancer and Michael sees the dream again and again and again in various incarnations, sometimes dying bravely to save his bride or children, sometimes living to their hundredth anniversary celebrating with all their thousands of progeny, children, grand and great great great grandchildren hugging them, cherishing them, cheering them and making love to Betsy just as passionately that night as ever and Michael writes a book on how to make a relationship work called "My Only Love" and it transforms the world, suddenly the economy strengthens, homelessness ends, everyone has full free health care, wars are a thing of the past because everyone is in love and all is good, with God, the eternal is now and Michael and Betsy are like Adam and Eve but this time they do not eat of the forbidden fruit, they only drink of one another and Eden returns, childbirth is painless and all are with God and immortal and blissful and then the dreams turn to the paranoid, a side Michael could never expunge and he gets hit by a garbage truck at thirty-five while Betsy looks on in horror, pregnant with twins, and she knows Michael will live on in her…. And then an unexplainable thing happens. Betsy and Michael start to share dreams. They wake up and excitedly recount their dreams to one another and invariably they are together in the dreams and happy and working to overcome some obstacle set out for them in the dream and they always manage to escape trouble. This goes on for three months. They spend almost every night together. They become as comfortable with themselves together as they are alone. Then they become even more comfortable together than alone. They not only dream alike. They think alike. Their friends tell them what a great couple they are. Lonnie is proud he introduced them and never lets them forget it which starts to annoy them a bit, though they are grateful. All the while, their professional lives are flourishing. Betsy has left acting altogether and is concentrating vigorously on her copywriting career. She writes some killer campaigns including the popular Gucci pocketbooks print ads targeted at, not so coincidentally psychologically, young mothers, which feature close-ups of beautiful young women with a Gucci bag slung over one shoulder and a smiling baby in the other arm and the headline, *Gucci Gucci*. Michael, in the meantime, dives into acting in a way he hadn't really ever before. Work at the newspaper is fine, but acting is his true passion. His big project is another one of Lonnie's monologues which he is extremely excited about though he doesn't lead on to anyone that he is, even Betsy, because something has opened up that is deeply personal within him, and though he shares everything with Betsy, he knows he must keep for himself this one thing, this love, this monologue, for he will give it to her only on the night of the first performance as his ultimate gesture of love. As he toils day and night, the vision of Betsy is what keeps him going in the grueling work of acting. He channels all the energy, passion of his love for Betsy into his second love, his acting, and through this he finds that Betsy is his life, Betsy, a love so real that it sends him beyond reality into boundless bliss. On the back of this bliss, the happy duo decide to move in together after just three and a half months, a move their parents, though they like each other's partners, feel is premature yet okay because things seem so right for the two. Their friends figure they're getting married anyway, so they don't think anything of it. And as it turns out things are fine. Just being in the same room makes them happy, so why not live in the same room for as long as possible given the temporality of life? The opening for Lonnie's new monologue arrives. Michael nears the end of the speech.

MICHAEL.   ... and I'm home with Darcy, Darcy my lovely, Darcy the tits, Darcy with wits and if she shits on me in my sleep I'll never ask for another favor again God. Oh God. Good. *(Michael stands alone on stage in dramatic pose. Sound of applause. Betsy claps.)*

OFFSTAGE VOICE.   Author! Author! *(Lonnie joins Michael on stage and they bow together. They hug.)*

NARRATOR.   Betsy and Michael say hi to everyone at the theater and thank them all so much for coming, and tell them how nice they all look, and it's so great for them to be supporting avant-garde theater, and see you at the next one. They leave the theater and go to a nearby cafe, The Mona Lisa. *(At table:)*

MICHAEL.   What'd you think?

BETSY.   I thought you were great.

MICHAEL.   But what did you think of the piece? *(She shrugs.)*

BETSY.   It was great.

MICHAEL.   You don't mean that.

BETSY.   Okay. I don't think it's my cup of tea.

MICHAEL.   What? It's too political or something?

BETSY.   No. Well, yeah, it's political, but ...

MICHAEL.   What? I don't care. I don't have any emotional investment in it. What?

BETSY.   I just didn't get it.

MICHAEL.   In what way?

BETSY.   Like on any level.

MICHAEL.   Yeah...? Go ahead. It's okay.

BETSY.   No, no, I'm sure it's just me, I'm not in the scene anymore, writing this mindless copy ...

MICHAEL.   I write mindless copy. It's okay, I really want to know what you thought.

BETSY.   Well, Lonnie's getting really obscure. I didn't understand most of the references and puns and plays and double and triple-entendres. I don't care about it. I just didn't get the point.

MICHAEL.   What kind of point were you looking for?

BETSY.   Well, he's so into the music of the language and not the meaning. It's like jazz. But it has no value beyond that. I don't learn anything new. It's just language junk. I'm used to narrative. I like a narrative, some kind of story. I know Lonnie doesn't ...

MICHAEL.   What about poetry? Do you like poetry that doesn't have a narrative?

BETSY.   Look, I'm sorry if this is upsetting you. You asked

39

for my opinion, and I'm trying to give it to you. You don't have to take apart every word I'm saying. I didn't like the monologue. I liked your performance, that's it, okay?

MICHAEL.   How could you like the performance if you didn't like the monologue?

BETSY.   What? I can't appreciate good acting?

MICHAEL.   That's like saying you hated the food, but you enjoyed your meal.

BETSY.   Give me a fucking break. Now you're just being absurd and touchy and stupid.

MICHAEL.   What? We're having a conversation. What happened?

BETSY.   Don't pull this shit. I didn't like the piece, okay? That's it. I'll tell fucking Lonnie myself, alright?

MICHAEL.   Alright.

BETSY.   Then good, that's what I'll do. I'll tell Lonnie I thought his monologue was pseudo-intellectual word games and not serious narrative.

MICHAEL.   You don't have to tell Lonnie that that goddamn piece isn't a narrative. Everyone in the fucking theater knows it wasn't a narrative. The people in this restaurant know it wasn't a narrative. You can ask anyone in the whole fucking city if they thought that fucking monologue was a narrative and they'd say no, no Betsy it wasn't a fucking narrative. You can search the planet until the day you die trying to find someone who thought that piece was a narrative and you'd never find a single person who thought so. You wanna know why? BECAUSE IT ISN'T A GODDAMN FUCKING NARRATIVE! But that's not the only way one might judge the piece. I mean I worked my goddamn ass off on that monologue. What the fuck do you think I've been doing the last two months?

BETSY.   You said you had no emotional investment.

MICHAEL.   Well, maybe I do.

BETSY.   Then why'd you say you don't?

MICHAEL.   You know you have a lot to learn about people.

BETSY.   Really?

MICHAEL.   You and your fucking narrative. Jesus! You didn't notice that I was staying up till two in the morning every goddamn night working on that thing? You think those words mean nothing to me? I'm just an actor, right? I'm not even an actor. I'm a lowly journalist who writes for a free paper ...

BETSY.   Oh my God ...

MICHAEL.   The words mean nothing to me, I don't even understand them. Well, I do. I own them. When I'm performing it they're my own whether it's a narrative or not.

BETSY.   You're being such an asshole.

MICHAEL.   I mean what's this? Are we in a narrative right now? Oh my God, we're not? This must be so boring. I mean I worked my fucking ass off and hoped that the woman I love could have some encouraging words, could share my excitement....

BETSY.   Michael, honey, shit, why didn't you tell me that the monologue meant so much...?

MICHAEL.   It meant a whole hell fuck of a lot, alright? It really did. *(Beat.)* My mother liked it.

BETSY.   That's it. You are such an insecure bastard. Need the approval of your mommy. You really do. And you need it from me too. Well I'm not your mommy. I'm sure your mommy loved the show just like she loves your brilliant theories about interactivity and the industrial revolution and all the other bullshit you spew. Who are you? What do you care about without worrying what other people think? Isn't it enough for you that *you* are happy with the monologue? Why do you have to impress others? Why should it matter what I think? What kind of fucked up purpose is it that you did the piece for me? I mean that's why you do everything. For others. You have to try to impress me that you're in good shape when you're not and you end up hurting yourself jogging. You take me to one of the fanciest restaurants in the city on our first date. It makes sense you're an actor, but do you love acting or performing?

MICHAEL.   Betsy, please, you're making a scene ...

BETSY.   Oh, you're embarrassed. I'm making a scene. What will people think? Fuck 'em. You could be such a good guy, Michael. You just have to learn to say, "Fuck you." Fuck you,

Lonnie. Fuck you, Mommy. Fuck you, Betsy. You know, Lonnie has more character than you'll ever have. He knows he's an asshole, doesn't try to make anyone think differently. I respect that in him. I really do. What do I respect in you? I mean, do you sleep with me to impress me that you can or because you love me? Is it us here now or is it the Michael show? You know what your problem is? You don't know who you are. That's really it. Are you an actor or a reporter? Are you your mother's son or your own man? Are you Lonnie's friend or my lover? Are you in love with me or yourself? YOUR MOTHER LIKED THE SHOW? GO HOME WITH HER! *(She turns to leave just as Lonnie arrives.)*

LONNIE.   Hey! Glad I caught you guys.

BETSY.   Lonnie, I thought your monologue sucked. I've always hated your writing even though I respect that you're an asshole. Goodnight! *(She storms off. Lonnie turns to Michael.)*

LONNIE.   They have food here? *(Choreographed scene of Michael and Betsy venting their rage and frustration to a hard rock beat. When their fury turns to exhaustion, the Narrator chimes in.)*

NARRATOR.   Betsy goes straight to Josie's apartment and stays there for the night. She thinks of calling Michael, but Josie stops her. Says he should sweat it out for the night, the bastard, then they could talk. Meanwhile, Michael is going nuts. He, of course, calls Josie's and Josie admits that Betsy is there, but says he can't talk to her and that he better think long and hard about what a shit he is. Michael says he will if he could just talk to Betsy, but Josie won't have it.

JOSIE.   *(Into phone.)* You better think long and hard about what a shit you are ... *(Beat. Continued into phone.)* I don't believe you. Good-bye, Michael. *(She slams the phone down. Turns to Betsy.)* You should be taking notes. Step one in troubled times with your man: PUNISH HIM. Now there are several ways of doing this. The best is *siege.* Let him sweat it out, go a little nutty, question everything he said and did. He'll get nice and worked up about it, bang his head on furniture, drink himself into misery, cry, curse, fight with Lonnie. Terrific. It's confusing for him. Men don't know how to handle this kind of treatment. Look at Stanley in *A Streetcar Named*

Desire. Big tough guy, right? His wife goes upstairs for a couple hours, visits her neighbors, guy goes nuts. *Stella! Stella!* Tennessee Williams understood his gender. The male brain can't process this kinda shit, not genetically programmed for it. It's all about control. Only one of you's gonna have it in a relationship, it may as well be you. If you go prancing back to the guy, he'll know it's okay to rant at you about his lousy acting and make you feel like shit. But if you torture him for a while, he'll live in fear of you leaving him again. PSYCHOLOGICAL TORTURE IS GOOD. It's great! And it's the best weapon we've got.

BETSY. I miss him.

JOSIE. Good! You feel like shit. If you didn't, there wouldn't be an issue. Step two: RELAX. You're the one in control. Think how he feels. He's turned into this pathetic runt begging to talk to you. Men are pitiable creatures when on their own, without their mate. Every second you put him off you're gaining valuable ground. He realizes how pathetic he is without you. It's too much of a *change* for him. Men can't handle change. Go to a cemetery. Look at the tombstones. Almost every time a woman dies, her husband is dead in a year. Woman's husband dies, no problem. She marries again, lives another couple decades in Florida, takes up shuffleboard, has a blast. Women adapt to change. We deal with it — cry like maniacs for a few days, curse our offenders, and move on. Men feel all sorry for themselves unable to believe this is their lot in life, like they're in some Greek tragedy. WHAT HAVE THEY DONE TO DESERVE SUCH A FATE? But they live in hope. Michael may be near death this very moment, but he's praying you'll give him one more chance. And he's ready to be a good little boy should he get it. You're going to be Queen Betsy. But for now, let him squirm.

BETSY. Easy for you to say. You have Butch.

JOSIE. That's right. But I've trained him. Step three: IT'S LIKE HOUSE BREAKING A DOG. You gotta be patient yet firm and invest the proper amount of time. You train 'em incorrectly, they shit all over you. Then they run away and get hit by a car.

43

BETSY. I feel like I've been hit by a car.

JOSIE. Multiply how you feel by a million and that's what our little Mikey's going through. They need us more than we need them. We're the only ones they really talk to about anything important. What do guys do when they get together? They throw a ball back and forth. Or they watch others throw balls back and forth. Or they *talk* about how others are throwing their balls. EVERYTHING MALE RELATES TO BALLS. They never really open up. All they know about each other is what teams they like and what sports they like to play. At parties, they sneak off to watch whatever game is on, and if they *do* talk, it's about whatever mindless activity they're involved with at the moment. Don't get me wrong — I love men. Butch is great. I am simply willing to accept the pathetic state of the male in our species and deal with what we're given.

BETSY. Fucking Lonnie's probably telling him to break up with me so they could hunt for women together like the good old days.

JOSIE. Not even Lonnie and his bullshit can break your hold on Michael. But when you do go back, it'll be with terms. The biggest mistake a general can make is to restore the enemy to full strength. In any battle, you must take land. You must seize the strategic high ground when your enemy is weak. Yes, you will go back my dear Betsy, but you will claim the spoils of war. And our desperate boy will nod his pretty head and kiss your toes. You and Michael are going to have a little talk. I'll take care of Lonnie.... *(Scene changes. Lonnie and Michael are in Michael's apartment. Michael looks terrible.)*

LONNIE. ... she'll come crawling back. They all do. Like an injured bird desperately clawing its way up the side of a tree. *(The phone rings.)* Voilà! *(Michael jumps and goes for it.)* Easy, partner. Cool. *(Michael picks up phone.)*

MICHAEL. Hello. *(Pause.)* Hi.

LONNIE. *(Whispering.)* Cool! Remain cool!

MICHAEL. Okay. You alright? *(Pause.)* Okay, bye. *(Michael hangs up.)*

LONNIE. Crawling back, huh?

MICHAEL. I don't know.

LONNIE.   What do you mean?

MICHAEL.   Said she wants to talk.

LONNIE.   *(Deadly serious.)* What'd you say?

MICHAEL.   I said okay.

LONNIE.   Wait, whoa, when? Where?

MICHAEL.   She's coming over.

LONNIE.   Now?

MICHAEL.   Yeah. *(Lonnie grabs the phone and puts it in Michael's hand.)*

LONNIE.   Call her back. Tell her not to come.

MICHAEL.   Why?

LONNIE.   You really don't know anything, do you?

MICHAEL.   I don't know what the hell you're talking about.

LONNIE.   Call her and say you can't do it now. Make up an excuse, anything, you have to take a bath, whatever.

MICHAEL.   I want to see her.

LONNIE.   Seeing her and *talking* to her are two extraordinarily different things, my friend. This is the most fundamental thing about women.

MICHAEL.   Yeah?

LONNIE.   YOU CAN'T TALK TO THEM!

MICHAEL.   I'm done taking your advice, Lonnie.

LONNIE.   When was the last time you won an argument with a woman? When? Never happens. Guys are no match for women when it comes to talking. We're overwhelmed, outclassed. We don't have a chance. Women, all they do since they're one-year-old is talk.

MICHAEL.   I'm not interested.

LONNIE.   My older sister, Sandra, all the time we're growing up, I'm always having my guy friends over, and what do we do? What did we do? WHAT DID WE DO?

MICHAEL.   Play ball, play war, games ...

LONNIE.   Exactly! But Sandra and her friends, it's like we were living in two different universes. All they ever did was lock themselves in Sandra's room and TALK. Every fucking time. It's all they did is talk. And when her friends weren't over, she was on the goddamn phone *talking* to them. When she turned twelve, my poor parents, who never had much

money, they had to get her her own phone, with *two* lines —
it was before all this call waiting crap and she'd go apeshit if
she missed a call, have an epileptic fit. After school, she'd be
in there talking, on the weekends, day and night, talking. Talk
talk talk. Sometimes, I didn't even know if there was anyone
in there with her or if she was on the phone or if she was
performing some weird babbling ritual. But it didn't matter.
It's the talk. I gotta tell you, after a while, it got fucking scary.
I mean she talked more in a six-month period than I think I
could ever talk in a goddamn lifetime. And I mean that. But
I thought it was just her, like she was some talk freak, had
some sick problem, disorder, was possessed by the devil or
some fucked up shit. But then I learned it's all of them, every fuckin' one of 'em, this intricate global network. All these
girls, women, these females talking and researching and
strategizing, sharing information, speculating, plotting. And
about what? What were they talking about? What *are* they talking about? WHAT? *(Michael shrugs.)* US! GUYS! If Betsy's on
her way over here to TALK, you don't stand a chance, buddy.
What'd *we* do last night? We had a bunch of beers while you
sulked. Didn't really talk, huh? Then today, more sulking,
couple beers, watched the Yankee game — just like when we
were kids. But now that we're grown up, we don't *play* sports,
we *watch* sports. Same difference except we don't get the car-
diovascular benefit. NOTHING CHANGES. Meantime, Betsy
and Josie, Josie that bitch, THAT MONSTER FUCKIN'
WHORE WHO ATE MANHATTAN — I'm not gonna go into
how she had the fucking gall to comment on my plays, like
she's some fuckin' postmodern fuckin' dramaturg with ques-
tions about plot ... I'm not gonna go into it — I can assure
you they have *not* been watching the Yankee game, they have
not been sulking, they have *not* been drinking beers. THEY'VE
BEEN PLANNING. Shit, Josie's the queen bitch of 'em all! She
may be the epicenter of all female horror. *(Beat.)*
MICHAEL. Do you just hate all women?
LONNIE. *(Shocked.)* What? Excuse me? Do I whah...? MY
PROBLEM IS I LOVE THEM ALL. I love everything about
them — their faces, their hair, their legs and breasts and

thighs and arms and fingers, their little stomachs, their skin, earlobes, and toes, ankles, teeth, tongues and breath and nurturing ways and sensitivity and tender touch. I LOVE *WOMAN*, all of them, I am humbled by them. I want to provide for them with all my passion, with every cell in my unworthy body, with my bones, my soul. I love them so, so much, sometimes I think I might go mad from my love, I might disappear in the vapor of my passion.... *(Lonnie, in tears, composes himself.)* Think of it this way. She is a tenth degree black belt, a killing machine; you are a little skinny first degree yellow belt. You're a bunny rabbit sniffing around a garden for a snack, she's a Tyrannosaurus Rex. DON'T TALK TO HER! My God, believe me, I've tried it. Remember Sueann?

MICHAEL.   From Kansas or somewhere in the midwest.

LONNIE.   Exactly! Some fuckin' midwestern bumpkin fuckin' place. Little prairie girl, right? She once wanted to talk. I thought I'd have a shot if I prepared. I was arrogant back then. Anyway, I stayed up all night. I made a list of a hundred irrefutable arguments about our relationship. All my points were air-tight. I had at least ten levels of defense mapped out for everything she could possibly come up with. I got all my lawyer buddies over to make sure every point was sound. I thought I was ready.

MICHAEL.   She destroyed you. You didn't write for a year. Started getting panic attacks. Almost lost your apartment.

LONNIE.   *(Gravely.)* It's like trying to keep up with Einstein in an argument about physics. Like fighting nuclear weapons with a slingshot. I learned my lesson. I suffered so you wouldn't have to. Women are just too advanced. Us guys will never catch up to their level in our lifetimes. It's mathematically impossible. All we could do is try to plant the seed of thought for future generations of guys so maybe a hundred years from now our great-grandsons might be able to talk on an even playing field, but we, our generation, it's too late for us. We have to take evasive action. We can't go head-to-head with women. We must *avoid* conversation. You think moose talk this shit over?

MICHAEL.   No more moose mating ...

LONNIE.   Moose sees a cute babe, taps a few times, fucks her. THAT'S A RELATIONSHIP.

MICHAEL.   *I* am not a moose!

LONNIE.   Yes you are. There's nothin' to *talk* about. You think *we'd* be *talking* about this shit if not for *them?* We get sucked into it, like some black hole, some vortex that saps all our sexual and creative energy into a void of useless chatter. LOOK AT US, MAN! Holed up talking. We've stooped to their level. We should be out there reproducing the species. We're men. Look what they've done to us. They've robbed us, they've robbed humanity. We've been ... violated. For God sakes man, call her. Tell her not to come. *(Michael hesitates. A door slams. Betsy and Josie enter. Lonnie screams in horror. Beat.)*

BETSY.   Hi. *(Music kicks in. Lonnie and Josie regard one another with disdain for a beat, then run off together. Michael and Betsy do choreographed routine to Narrator's speech.)*

NARRATOR.   Betsy and Michael talk, or rather, Betsy talks and Michael listens. Michael admits he was wrong and apologizes and swears he'll never be so petty again. They hug and kiss and proclaim their love for one another over and over again. They make love that night more passionately than ever. They each think that maybe their relationship has vaulted to a new, greater level. But when morning comes, they both sense something has changed. Some invisible thread that once bound them has snapped. Though they try, they cannot go back to the way things had been. Like Sisyphus and his rock, they can no longer reside for more than a moment on the mountain top. Six months pass. Their life together becomes routine. They develop habits. Before going to sleep, Betsy always brushes her teeth first, then shortly thereafter, Michael does so. They read books in bed till they fall asleep. They make love just once a week, always in the missionary position, after reading, and it is only once a month that their lovemaking is actually exciting. The rest of the time it is to satisfy the other and to convince themselves that everything is okay. They sit together in the morning and talk about the news in the Times. Michael always eats Special K cereal with milk and a sprinkle of cinnamon. Betsy eats a piece of toast and drinks coffee which she brews in the cute little one-cup plunger coffee maker Josie gave them when they moved in together. They become a real team. Each rarely refers to him or herself as "I." It is always "we." *We're* going to a movie tonight. We're going to the Cape for the weekend. We're not happy with the lack of water pressure in our apartment. We think the situation in the city's schools stinks. We aren't sleeping well. We're not the same as we used to be. We've changed. We're not as happy.... They kiss good-bye in the morning and hello in the evening, but the kiss is not sexual or flirtatious. It's like a handshake. It's no more personal than when they kiss their friends hello. The kisses are dry, closed-mouthed. They don't think of them as kisses. They don't think about them at all as it is such a ritual, like flushing the toilet. It's just something they do, like when one calls the other and says, "How are you?" and the other says, "Fine." And since their kisses are only a means of saying hello, a rote greeting, they become simply an extension of rhetorical thoughtless language, with no tangible, physical effect so that in the seconds the kisses occur, it is as if the kissers are momentarily dead.... They get to the point where they never lock the bathroom door. They share the small room no matter what activity each is engaged in. Betsy doesn't tell Michael, but she isn't crazy about this arrangement. She'd like her privacy sometimes, but she doesn't want Michael to think it's a reflection on their relationship which she realizes is stupid, she should talk to him, but she just doesn't want to bring it up. Michael has no idea Betsy feels this way. Seeing Betsy sitting on the toilet is no different to Michael than seeing her sitting at the kitchen table. Seeing each other clothed is no different than being naked together. Touching one another is no different than talking on the phone. When making love, they may as well be sleeping — which they'd rather be doing except for that one time a month when they get off on it. But they have developed *compassion* for one another. Compassion, a deep sense of respect and pity ... that intangible something which binds them, which forces them to remain a couple. When Betsy comes home from a tough day, Michael holds her and is genuinely concerned about her. He wishes she would be happy, and, in his arms, she is comforted. Similarly, when Michael faces disappointment, he looks to Betsy for support and she is always, happily, there for him. At such times, they often talk about themselves as a team up against the world. It's nice to know they have one another. As they independently consider and shudder at the thought of their seemingly inevitable breakup, it is the fear of ripping apart their compassionate bond that makes them try to convince themselves that things will work out. And on the surface, all is fine. *(In bed:)*

BETSY.   What were you like as a kid?

MICHAEL.   Probably not much different than I am now. Except now I actually have sex instead of constantly fantasizing about it.

BETSY.   Which is better, the fantasy or the reality?

MICHAEL.   I guess they both have their up and down sides.

BETSY.   Honest answer.

MICHAEL.   I try.

BETSY.   Do you think we would have gotten along as kids?

MICHAEL.   Sure.

BETSY.   Good.

MICHAEL.   So I think we should get married.

BETSY.   Excuse me?

MICHAEL.   What, you don't agree?

BETSY.   I'm just shocked.

MICHAEL.   Makes sense, doesn't it? I mean is it really such a surprise?

BETSY.   It's a bit of a surprise.

MICHAEL.   Well, what do couples do? There's only two choices. Get married or break up. I say we get married.

BETSY.   So that's it? Choice "A" and choice "B". Door number one or door number two.

MICHAEL.   I didn't think this would upset you. I'm sorry.

BETSY.   Do you really think this is the time to consider marriage?

MICHAEL.   I'd like to commit.

BETSY.   We have serious problems, Michael.

MICHAEL.   I know.

BETSY. I don't think marriage will solve them.

MICHAEL. What do you think will?

BETSY. I don't know that anything will. Some problems can't be solved I guess.

MICHAEL. So you think we should break up?

BETSY. I don't know what I think. Do I have to come up with an answer now?

MICHAEL. It's kind of important, don't you think?

BETSY. What's going on here, Michael?

MICHAEL. I asked you to marry me.

BETSY. I know, but what's going on, goddamnit? I mean we really have to talk about some serious issues and you're just leaping over this huge chasm which is the reality of our relationship and saying, screw it, let's just get married and then worry about the fact that the passion we used to have left us months ago. *(Silence.)*

MICHAEL. Maybe we should hold off on this conversation. Love you.

BETSY. I love you, too.

MICHAEL. Want to hear exciting news?

BETSY. Sure.

MICHAEL. Lonnie and I are going skydiving next week.

BETSY. What?

MICHAEL. Lonnie and I are going skydiving.

BETSY. I heard you. I'm just surprised.

MICHAEL. Lonnie thought it would be a good experience for artists. I agree.

BETSY. Really? I thought you weren't interested in that kind of stuff.

MICHAEL. What do you mean?

BETSY. On our first date, you told me you don't need that kind of artificial stimulation in your life.

MICHAEL. What's the big deal? It'll be fun.

BETSY. How'd it come up?

MICHAEL. We were taking a rehearsal break and he mentioned it. What do you mean *how*? *(Scene transforms. Betsy speaks as Michael and Lonnie are now aboard a plane huddled together, preparing for the jump.)*

BETSY. You're leaving me, aren't you? You're asking me to marry you because you're afraid to do what you really want which is to break up. And you want *me* to be the one to say, "We gotta talk." *(Michael and Lonnie jump. They fall during the rest of Betsy's speech.)* I'm not stupid. I know what's going on. And now you're going to jump out of a goddamn airplane because I somehow don't fulfill your quota, your threshold of excitement anymore and you're too weak to just leave me! I mean, maybe you're not as you appear. Maybe *we're* not. Maybe nothing is. But I see what you're doing. You want out of us, but you can't bring yourself to actually do it because, as usual, you're scared. Scared of loneliness, scared of me, scared of making a decision. You can't take responsibility for a bold action. And maybe I'm in the same situation but hold out hope. Hope that our relationship isn't dying when it may already be dead. Why did we die Michael? What happened? Guess it could have been anything, may never know. Like when people die. Lots of specific causes, but ultimately all people die for the same reason — lack of oxygen to the brain. Whether they have a heart attack or cancer or get hit by a car or die in a fire, the cause of death is always lack of oxygen to the brain. I guess, ultimately, we ended for the same reason all couples do: lack of will to stay together. It just really sucks. It sucks that we didn't make it. It sucks that you ultimately need Lonnie more than me, which, whether you believe this or not, I understand and appreciate. I do. You and Lonnie have a history. You and I have a *limited* history. And I'm so goddamn jealous of Lonnie for that. And I'm sorry for you. And me. Because we could have had a long enough history to make it. We almost did. It's all luck of circumstance. We just didn't have enough luck and that's life. Politics. Lonnie writes his pathetic version — which maybe somehow is more real than anything. We live ours. It's the same fuckin' thing, the same game. Life is all one big interactive game, huh? And if I don't like it ... I could take it up with God. *(Michael and Lonnie land safely, exhilarated, and hug. Final scene: Betsy and Michael exchange lines from their first Asides at the top of the show. These are not imitations of the earlier deliveries. They are echoes.)* Shit, he's cute.

MICHAEL.   Wow, I feel chemistry here.

BETSY.   I actually feel the emptiness between my legs.

MICHAEL.   I mean I feel the possibility of an absence.

BETSY.   I could just put my hands on his cheek, his neck, that tender skin.

MICHAEL.   Like cold is the absence of heat. Or is it absinthe?

BETSY.   I could whisper, "Wanna come back to my place for some fun?"

MICHAEL.   No, absence. *(They turn and face one another and continue their monologues, now overlapping. Overlapping Betsy.)* The absence of misery, loneliness, suffering. The chance to not wake up hugging dreams of my sweet ex Lisa. Seven fucking years ago, destroyed me and left me shopping for fruit alone at four in the morning and going to these fucking plays at all hours. I hate plays that I don't star in. It's just the hope of maybe bumping into a beautiful woman that keeps me coming back and back for months, years already and now, right now, she is next to me.

BETSY.   *(Overlapping Michael.)* I could trace his bones with my fingers.... God, that strong but gentle thing unravels me, opens me, oh God I could just hug him, I could just fuck him, I want to get laid or at least touch a man.... Shit, he probably lives with his girlfriend, some beautiful bitch who keeps him on a leash and only lets him out to send on errands. Else he's heavy into S&M and wants to tie me up and spank me on the first date. I hate that shit on the first date. *(The glorious loud music, heard during the scene when they met, kicks in and Michael and Betsy continue in slow motion, mouthing words though they cannot be heard. Then the music cuts out and they continue in slow motion, gently attempting to make contact, though they cannot. Michael and Betsy continue as Lonnie and Josie appear. They address the audience.)*

LONNIE.   I never liked her. Couldn't tell you because I had enormous respect for you and the relationship. You know that.

I wouldn't dream of interfering.

JOSIE. I never liked the guy. I could tell you that now. Believe me, you could do better. I think his hair loss is accelerating. Guy's gonna be a cue-ball head.

LONNIE. Count yourself among the lucky, pal. A weaker man might've married her.

JOSIE. I mean there are two and a half billion guys out there. There's gotta be one more for you — maybe.

LONNIE. I bet she's gay. Fuckin' lesbo. Which is fine. I like lesbians. They present some interesting possibilities. But you don't wanna get involved in that shit.

JOSIE. I think he's gay. In love with Lonnie. I'm serious. I've seen it happen. Better to get out now than find out three kids later.

LONNIE. Okay. Fallacy number one about breaking up: You need time before moving on. That's bullshit. The best medicine is to fuck another girl immediately. Within hours if possible. I'm serious.

JOSIE. Step one after breaking up: Cry your fucking head off. Get it all out. Expel the demons.

LONNIE. Fallacy number two: Make it a clean break. Again, bullshit. If she's willing to jump back in the sack, go for it. Cuts the pain.

JOSIE. Step two: Forget he ever existed. If necessary, there are hypnotists who specialize in these cases.

LONNIE. It's like moose. Or wait a sec. You know what? All this moose mating stuff. Funny, someone pointed out to me it actually isn't moose that do that shit. I got it mixed up. I think it's caribou … or reindeer … whatever. The point is … what was the point? I lost my train of thought here. Forget it. Let's watch the Yankee game fergodsakes. It's goddamn exhausting talking about all this bullshit.

JOSIE. Listen, I don't know if this is the best time to tell you this, but I'm leaving Butch. Lonnie and I are getting back together. With me and Lon, it's a fair fight. We're well matched.

LONNIE. What can I say? I'm in love. She's a great sparring partner. *(Over-the-top romantic music kicks in as Lonnie and Josie sweep into one another's arms in front of the distraught Michael and Betsy. Lonnie dips Josie, and they tenderly kiss and swoon as the music swells. On screen projected over final tableau in fancy lettering: THE END. Lights fade.)*

THE END

PROPERTY LIST

Duffel bag (BETSY)
Scrap of paper (MICHAEL)
Pen (MICHAEL)
Telephones
TV remote control (LONNIE)
Football (LONNIE)
Cash (BETSY)
Two books (BETSY, MICHAEL)
Video game joystick (LONNIE)
Bong (LONNIE)
Match (LONNIE)

SOUND EFFECTS

Applause
Thunder
Call-waiting tone
Phone rings

NEW PLAYS

★ **HONOUR by Joanna Murray-Smith.** In a series of intense confrontations, a wife, husband, lover and daughter negotiate the forces of passion, history, responsibility and honour. "HONOUR makes for surprisingly interesting viewing. Tight, crackling dialogue (usually played out in punchy verbal duels) captures characters unable to deal with emotions ... Murray-Smith effectively places her characters in situations that strip away pretense." *–Variety* "... the play's virtues are strong: a distinctive theatrical voice, passionate concerns ... HONOUR might just capture a few honors of its own." *–Time Out Magazine* [1M, 3W] ISBN: 0-8222-1683-3

★ **MR. PETERS' CONNECTIONS by Arthur Miller.** Mr. Miller describes the protagonist as existing in a dream-like state when the mind is "freed to roam from real memories to conjectures, from trivialities to tragic insights, from terror of death to glorying in one's being alive." With this memory play, the Tony Award and Pulitzer Prize-winner reaffirms his stature as the world's foremost dramatist. "... a cross between Joycean stream-of-consciousness and Strindberg's dream plays, sweetened with a dose of William Saroyan's philosophical whimsy ... CONNECTIONS is most intriguing ..." *–The NY Times* [5M, 3W] ISBN: 0-8222-1687-6

★ **THE WAITING ROOM by Lisa Loomer.** Three women from different centuries meet in a doctor's waiting room in this dark comedy about the timeless quest for beauty – and its cost. "... THE WAITING ROOM ... is a bold, risky melange of conflicting elements that is ... terrifically moving ... There's no resisting the fierce emotional pull of the play." *–The NY Times* "... one of the high points of this year's Off-Broadway season ... THE WAITING ROOM is well worth a visit." *–Back Stage* [7M, 4W, flexible casting] ISBN: 0-8222-1594-2

★ **THE OLD SETTLER by John Henry Redwood.** A sweet-natured comedy about two church-going sisters in 1943 Harlem and the handsome young man who rents a room in their apartment. "For all of its decent sentiments, THE OLD SETTLER avoids sentimentality. It has the authenticity and lack of pretense of an Early American sampler." *–The NY Times* "We've had some fine plays Off-Broadway this season, and this is one of the best." *–The NY Post* [1M, 3W] ISBN: 0-8-222-1642-6

★ **LAST TRAIN TO NIBROC by Arlene Hutton.** In 1940 two young strangers share a seat on a train bound east only to find their paths will cross again. "All aboard. LAST TRAIN TO NIBROC is a sweetly told little chamber romance." *–Show Business* "... [a] gently charming little play, reminiscent of Thornton Wilder in its look at rustic Americans who are to be treasured for their simplicity and directness ..." *–Associated Press* "The old formula of boy wins girls, boy loses girl, boy wins girl still works ... [a] well-made play that perfectly captures a slice of small-town-life-gone-by." *–Back Stage* [1M, 1W] ISBN: 0-8222-1753-8

★ **OVER THE RIVER AND THROUGH THE WOODS by Joe DiPietro.** Nick sees both sets of his grandparents every Sunday for dinner. This is routine until he has to tell them that he's been offered a dream job in Seattle. The news doesn't sit so well. "A hilarious family comedy that is even funnier than his long running musical revue *I Love You, You're Perfect, Now Change*." *–Back Stage* "Loaded with laughs every step of the way." *–Star-Ledger* [3M, 3W] ISBN: 0-8222-1712-0

★ **SIDE MAN by Warren Leight.** 1999 Tony Award winner. This is the story of a broken family and the decline of jazz as popular entertainment. "... a tender, deeply personal memory play about the turmoil in the family of a jazz musician as his career crumbles at the dawn of the age of rock-and-roll ..." *–The NY Times* "[SIDE MAN] is an elegy for two things – a lost world and a lost love. When the two notes sound together in harmony, it is moving and graceful ..." *–The NY Daily News* "An atmospheric memory play ... with crisp dialogue and clearly drawn characters ... reflects the passing of an era with persuasive insight ... The joy and despair of the musicians is skillfully illustrated." *–Variety* [5M, 3W] ISBN: 0-8222-1721-X

DRAMATISTS PLAY SERVICE, INC.
440 Park Avenue South, New York, NY 10016 212-683-8960 Fax 212-213-1539
postmaster@dramatists.com www.dramatists.com

NEW PLAYS

★ **CLOSER by Patrick Marber.** Winner of the 1998 Olivier Award for Best Play and the 1999 New York Drama Critics Circle Award for Best Foreign Play. Four lives intertwine over the course of four and a half years in this densely plotted, stinging look at modern love and betrayal. "CLOSER is a sad, savvy, often funny play that casts a steely, unblinking gaze at the world of relationships and lets you come to your own conclusions ... CLOSER does not merely hold your attention; it burrows into you." –*New York Magazine* "A powerful, darkly funny play about the cosmic collision between the sun of love and the comet of desire." –*Newsweek Magazine* [2M, 2W] ISBN: 0-8222-1722-8

★ **THE MOST FABULOUS STORY EVER TOLD by Paul Rudnick.** A stage manager, headset and prompt book at hand, brings the house lights to half, then dark, and cues the creation of the world. Throughout the play, she's in control of everything. In other words, she's either God, or she thinks she is. "Line by line, Mr. Rudnick may be the funniest writer for the stage in the United States today ... One-liners, epigrams, withering put-downs and flashing repartee: These are the candles that Mr. Rudnick lights instead of cursing the darkness ... a testament to the virtues of laughing ... and in laughter, there is something like the memory of Eden." –*The NY Times* "Funny it is ... consistently, rapaciously, deliriously ... easily the funniest play in town." –*Variety* [4M, 5W] ISBN: 0-8222-1720-1

★ **A DOLL'S HOUSE by Henrik Ibsen, adapted by Frank McGuinness.** Winner of the 1997 Tony Award for Best Revival. "New, raw, gut-twisting and gripping. Easily the hottest drama this season." –*USA Today* "Bold, brilliant and alive." –*The Wall Street Journal* "A thunderclap of an evening that takes your breath away." –*Time Magazine* [4M, 4W, 2 boys] ISBN: 0-8222-1636-1

★ **THE HERBAL BED by Peter Whelan.** The play is based on actual events which occurred in Stratford-upon-Avon in the summer of 1613, when William Shakespeare's elder daughter was publicly accused of having a sexual liaison with a married neighbor and family friend. "In his probing new play, THE HERBAL BED ... Peter Whelan muses about a sidelong event in the life of Shakespeare's family and creates a finely textured tapestry of love and lies in the early 17th-century Stratford." –*The NY Times* "It is a first rate drama with interesting moral issues of truth and expediency." –*The NY Post* [5M, 3W] ISBN: 0-8222-1675-2

★ **SNAKEBIT by David Marshall Grant.** A study of modern friendship when put to the test. "... a rather smart and absorbing evening of water-cooler theater, the intimate sort of Off-Broadway experience that has you picking apart the recognizable characters long after the curtain calls." – *The NY Times* "Off-Broadway keeps on presenting us with compelling reasons for going to the theater. The latest is SNAKEBIT, David Marshall Grant's smart new comic drama about being thirtysomething and losing one's way in life." –*The NY Daily News* [3M, 1W] ISBN: 0-8222-1724-4

★ **A QUESTION OF MERCY by David Rabe.** The Obie Award-winning playwright probes the sensitive and controversial issue of doctor-assisted suicide in the age of AIDS in this poignant drama. "There are many devastating ironies in Mr. Rabe's beautifully considered, piercingly clear-eyed work ..." –*The NY Times* "With unsettling candor and disturbing insight, the play arouses pity and understanding of a troubling subject ... Rabe's provocative tale is an affirmation of dignity that rings clear and true." –*Variety* [6M, 1W] ISBN: 0-8222-1643-4

★ **DIMLY PERCEIVED THREATS TO THE SYSTEM by Jon Klein.** Reality and fantasy overlap with hilarious results as this unforgettable family attempts to survive the nineties. "Here's a play whose point about fractured families goes to the heart, mind – and ears." –*The Washington Post* "... an end-of-the millennium comedy about a family on the verge of a nervous breakdown ... Trenchant and hilarious ..." –*The Baltimore Sun* [2M, 4W] ISBN: 0-8222-1677-9

DRAMATISTS PLAY SERVICE, INC.
440 Park Avenue South, New York, NY 10016 212-683-8960 Fax 212-213-1539
postmaster@dramatists.com www.dramatists.com

NEW PLAYS

★ **AS BEES IN HONEY DROWN by Douglas Carter Beane.** Winner of the John Gassner Playwriting Award. A hot young novelist finds the subject of his new screenplay in a New York socialite who leads him into the world of *Auntie Mame* and *Breakfast at Tiffany's*, before she takes him for a ride. "A delicious soufflé of a satire ... [an] extremely entertaining fable for an age that always chooses image over substance." *—The NY Times* "... A witty assessment of one of the most active and relentless industries in a consumer society ... the creation of 'hot' young things, which the media have learned to mass produce with efficiency and zeal." *—The NY Daily News* [3M, 3W, flexible casting] ISBN: 0-8222-1651-5

★ **STUPID KIDS by John C. Russell.** In rapid, highly stylized scenes, the story follows four high-school students as they make their way from first through eighth period and beyond, struggling with the fears, frustrations, and longings peculiar to youth. "In STUPID KIDS ... playwright John C. Russell gets the opera of adolescence to a T ... The stylized teenspeak of STUPID KIDS ... suggests that Mr. Russell may have hidden a tape recorder under a desk in study hall somewhere and then scoured the tapes for good quotations ... it is the kids' insular, ceaselessly churning world, a pre-adult world of Doritos and libidos, that the playwright seeks to lay bare." *—The NY Times* "STUPID KIDS [is] a sharp-edged ... whoosh of teen angst and conformity anguish. It is also very funny." *—NY Newsday* [2M, 2W] ISBN: 0-8222-1698-1

★ **COLLECTED STORIES by Donald Margulies.** From Obie Award-winner Donald Margulies comes a provocative analysis of a student-teacher relationship that turns sour when the protégé becomes a rival. "With his fine ear for detail, Margulies creates an authentic, insular world, and he gives equal weight to the opposing viewpoints of two formidable characters." *—The LA Times* "This is probably Margulies' best play to date ..." *—The NY Post* "... always fluid and lively, the play is thick with ideas, like a stock-pot of good stew." *—The Village Voice* [2W] ISBN: 0-8222-1640-X

★ **FREEDOMLAND by Amy Freed.** An overdue showdown between a son and his father sets off fireworks that illuminate the neurosis, rage and anxiety of one family – and of America at the turn of the millennium. "FREEDOMLAND's more obvious links are to *Buried Child* and *Bosoms and Neglect*. Freed, like Guare, is an inspired wordsmith with a gift for surreal touches in situations grounded in familiar and real territory." *—Curtain Up* [3M, 4W] ISBN: 0-8222-1719-8

★ **STOP KISS by Diana Son.** A poignant and funny play about the ways, both sudden and slow, that lives can change irrevocably. "There's so much that is vital and exciting about STOP KISS ... you want to embrace this young author and cheer her onto other works ... the writing on display here is funny and credible ... you also will be charmed by its heartfelt characters and up-to-the-minute humor." *—The NY Daily News* "... irresistibly exciting ... a sweet, sad, and enchantingly sincere play." *—The NY Times* [3M, 3W] ISBN: 0-8222-1731-7

★ **THREE DAYS OF RAIN by Richard Greenberg.** The sins of fathers and mothers make for a bittersweet elegy in this poignant and revealing drama. "... a work so perfectly judged it heralds the arrival of a major playwright ... Greenberg is extraordinary." *—The NY Daily News* "Greenberg's play is filled with graceful passages that are by turns melancholy, harrowing, and often, quite funny." *—Variety* [2M, 1W] ISBN: 0-8222-1676-0

★ **THE WEIR by Conor McPherson.** In a bar in rural Ireland, the local men swap spooky stories in an attempt to impress a young woman from Dublin who recently moved into a nearby "haunted" house. However, the tables are soon turned when she spins a yarn of her own. "You shed all sense of time at this beautiful and devious new play." *—The NY Times* "Sheer theatrical magic. I have rarely been so convinced that I have just seen a modern classic. Tremendous." *—The London Daily Telegraph* [4M, 1W] ISBN: 0-8222-1706-6

DRAMATISTS PLAY SERVICE, INC.
440 Park Avenue South, New York, NY 10016 212-683-8960 Fax 212-213-1539
postmaster@dramatists.com   www.dramatists.com